Mel Bay Presents
English Carols
for
Piano Solo

By Gail Smith

Cover Photo Credit: H. Armstrong Roberts
4203 Locust Street, Philadelphia, PA 19104

A cassette tape of the music in this book is now available. The publisher strongly recommends the use of this cassette tape along with the text to insure accuracy of interpretation and ease in learning.

Foreword

A carol is a song of joy originally accompanying a dance.

The word "carol" is derived from the Italian "carola," a ring-dance, from "carolare," to sing.

The word "carol" has been in use in England for at least some seven hundred years. An old proverb says:

> "The French sing or pipe,
> The Spaniards wail,
> The Germans howl,
> The Italians caper
> and the English carol."

May your Christmas season be enriched by playing and listening to these twenty-five new piano arrangements of English carols.

GAIL SMITH

Table of Contents

Deck The Halls

Very little is known about this lively carol, but it is quite old. Mozart even used its melody in a violin and piano duet composed around 1700. In Merry Olde England it was the custom to deck the vast, vaulted halls at Christmastime with wreaths, flowers and holly.

Arr. by Gail Smith

Masters In The Hall

The English compiler of Christmas carols, Edmund Sedding was organist of Chartres Cathedral. He asked William Morris (1834-1896) to write some verses to fit this tune. Morris recaptured the medieval flavor in this text and Sedding published it in 1860 in his *Ancient Christmas Carols*.

William Morris, ca. 1860

Carol from Chartres
Arr. by Gail Smith

7

The Boar's Head Carol

Many Boar's Head carols have come down to us from the Middle Ages. In fact, the earliest carol to appear in print was "The Boar's Head" in Wynken de Worde's collection of *Christmasse Carolles*, published in 1521. The serving of this delicacy on Christmas Day was a widespread practice. The ushering in of the boar's head with the singing of this carol was the custom during Christmas dinner.

Arr. by Gail Smith

9

The Bellman's Carol

It is believed that Shakespeare refers to this carol in *As You Like It*, ". . . this carol they began that hour with a hey, and a ho, and hey nonino." Cecil Sharpe included this carol in one of his many collections. Sharpe did much research of early English folk music and carols.

Arr. by Gail Smith

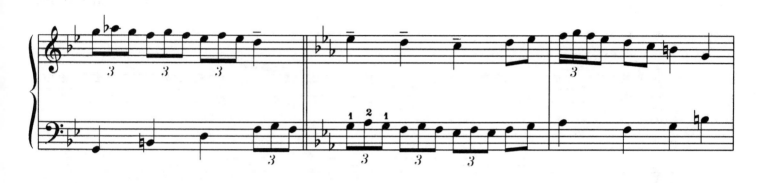

The First Nowell

This old English carol is considered a cento. What this means is that it is a musical work made up of passages from other compositions. The first known printed version of this carol was in William Sandys' *Christmas Carols Ancient and Modern*, published in 1833. Sandys was born in London in 1792 and died there in 1874. He was a lawyer, yet had musical interests and did much to preserve and create interest in carols. Together with Charles Dickens he did much to restore interest in the celebration of Christmas as a Christian festival in England. Parliament had forbidden its observance in 1644 and although the feast was revived by Charles II, it did not fully take on its Christian significance until the dawn of the nineteenth century.

Arr. by Gail Smith

Sussex Carol

"On Christmas night all Christians sing to hear the news the angels bring."

The melody and text to this carol were taken down probably by Cecil Sharpe as he heard it sung by Mrs. Verrall, Monks Gate, Sussex. It was published in Cecil Sharpe's *English Folk-Carols, No. X*

Arr. by Gail Smith

Gloucestershire Wassail

A special custom was observed in connection with this carol in Gloucestershire, England going back over a hundred years. A group of carolers paraded through the streets carrying a huge bowl decorated with ribbons and filled with spiced ale. As the carolers sang, they served the wassail, so it was "Wassail, all over the town!"

Arr. by Gail Smith

Here We Come A Wassailing

This tune from Yorkshire was popularized by Sir John Stainer:

"Love and joy come to you
And to you your wassail too,
And God Bless you, and send you
A happy New Year."

If the wassailing was done formally, the wassail procession visited the principal orchards of the parish, caroling on the way. In each orchard major trees were selected and the roots sprinkled with the wassail. After the toast ". . .to the health and prosperity of a friend," everyone enjoyed drinking the wonderful wassail. The drink consisted of ale or mulled cider sweetened with sugar, and flavored with nutmeg, cinnamon, cloves, roasted apples, and perhaps egg.

Yorkshire Carol
Arr. by Gail Smith

While Shepherds Watched Their Flocks

This carol was written by Nahum Tate (1652-1715). He was poet laureate of England at the time.

Arr. by Gail Smith

This Endris Night

This is a lullaby carol. The title means, "the other night," or "several nights ago." The words originate from manuscript carols of the late Middle Ages.

Arr. by Gail Smith

Away In A Manger

The melody to this beautiful carol was composed by William James Kirkpatrick (1838-1921). He was musical director at Grace Methodist Episcopal Church in Philadelphia after coming to America. He published over 80 song collections.

Arr. by Gail Smith

Chester Carol Lullaby

Of all the early English carols, one of the most beautiful is a processional lullaby sung by the nuns of St. Mary's, Chester. This Chester carol dates from circa 1425. English carols have been classified according to their subject matter. The early ones are those of the Nativity and the Incarnation, together with a large group dealing with the Annunciation.

circa 1425
Arr. by Gail Smith

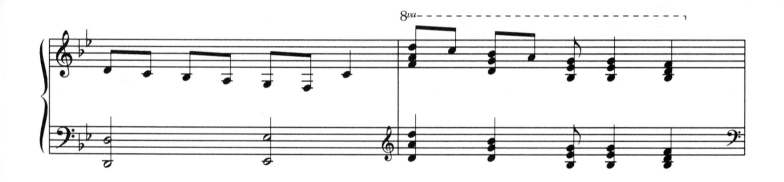

Coventry Carol

This carol was included in the famous pageant of the *Sherman and Tailors' Guilds*, a mystery play performed in Coventry, England, as early as the fifteenth century. Many members of the English royal family witnessed the presentation, among them were: Margaret the Queen of Henry VI in 1456, Richard III in 1484, and Henry VII in 1492. In the pageant, the carol is sung by the women of Bethlehem just before their children are killed by Herod's soldiers.

Arr. by Gail Smith

Once In Royal David's City

This carol is one from Mrs. Cecil Frances Alexander's *Hymns for Little Children*, published in 1848. Each of the hymns in her book was designed to teach the catechism. They were based on the words of the Apostles' Creed: "Was conceived of the Holy Ghost, born of the Virgin Mary." The words were linked with Dr. Gauntlett's tune.

Arr. by Gail Smith

What Child Is This?

Sir John Stainer (1840-1901) is responsible for the popularizing of this carol. Stainer was a distinguished composer and organist who began his musical training as a chorister at Saint Paul's Cathedral in London when he was seven years old. Queen Victoria knighted him in 1888 for his musical contributions to England.

The words to this carol were written by William Dix. Stainer adapted an ancient Irish jig, "Greensleeves," to fit the text and thus arranged and popularized this favorite carol of Englishmen.

Arr. by Gail Smith

31

In The Bleak Midwinter

This literary gem was first used as a hymn in the *English Hymnal*, 1906. "Cranham" was written by Gustav Holst for this hymn and is as simple and unpretentious as the words. Holst was born at Cheltenham, England on September 21, 1874 and died in London on May 25, 1934. He was a composer, teacher and organist. Holst taught composition at the Royal College of Music.

Arr. by Gail Smith

As With Gladness Men Of Old

This epiphany hymn was first published in *Hymns of Love and Joy*, 1861. William Dix, the noted Englishman, was author of the text. He earned his living as the manager of a marine insurance company in Bristol. In his spare time he wrote many fine hymns.

Traditional
Arr. by Gail Smith

Good Christian Men, Rejoice

This fourteenth century melody was arranged by the Englishman John Stainer. John Mason Neale (1818-1866) translated the text and it appeared in Neale's *Carols for Christmastide*, printed in 1853. This carol is derived from the macaronic carol "In dulci jubilo," which was translated by John Wadderburn in 1567.

Arr. by Gail Smith

God Rest Ye Merry, Gentlemen

In *A Christmas Carol*, Charles Dickens explains how Scrooge was busy in his country house on Christmas Eve when a half-starved youth stopped by to sing him a carol. Dickens wrote, "At the first sound of 'God rest you merry, gentlemen, Let nothing you dismay,' Scrooge seized the ruler with such energy of action that the singer flew in terror."

Arr. by Gail Smith

The Holly And The Ivy

During the middle ages the two plants—holly and ivy—were associated with the sexes, holly being masculine and ivy feminine. This 15th century carol is cheerful yet devotional and may symbolize redemption by the blossom, berry, thorns and bark of the holly tree.

Arr. by Gail Smith

I Saw Three Ships

There is a large class of folksong carols based mainly on subjects drawn from mystery plays and pageants. Among these is "I Saw Three Ships." Cecil Sharpe is credited with taking this carol down in Worchestershire. Sharpe was born in London on November 22, 1859, and died there June 23, 1924. His father was a city merchant whose hobby was architecture. Young Cecil branched into a love of art, dance and music. In 1911 Cecil Sharpe founded the English Folk-Dance Society for the revival of the arts.

Arr. by Gail Smith

Good King Wenceslas

This tune was originally a spring-carol, "Tempus adest Floridum" published in 1582 in an interesting and unique volume, *Piæ cantiones*, compiled by Theodoric Peter of Nylandt. Dr. J. M. Neale wrote an entirely new text for this tune based on an old legend about Saint Wenceslas. Yes, there actually was a noble man Wenceslas. He wasn't a king, however, but the Duke of Bohemia, now known as Czechoslovakia. Although he was a very good person, unfortunately he was murdered in 929 by his jealous younger brother. Neale used this martyred Wenceslas as the subject for this children's Christmas carol as an example of a very generous person.

Arr. by Gail Smith

Patapan

This carol appeared in *Noels Bourgignons de Bernard de la Monnoye*, 1842. Bernard wrote many lively songs and carols.

Arr. by Gail Smith

The Twelve Days Of Christmas

Eight maids a-milking, ten lords a-leaping are expressions of traditional Christianity? How on earth?

Well, here's how. In 16th century England after the accession of Elizabeth I the English who remained loyal to Roman Catholicism found themselves on the wrong side of the law. They were forbidden by royal decree to teach the catechism to their children, so they disguised catechistic teachings in metaphors and put them to a tune. The twelve days of Christmas is one of those resulting songs. The carol veils truths about Christ's life and message.

The singer of the carol is an ordinary person who believes in Christ, and his or her "true love" is God the Father. The accumulative pattern of going back each time through all the verses teaches the on-going and abundant blessings of a loving God.

The partridge, a bird reputed to choose death to defend its young, is an ancient Christian symbol of Christ. The two turtle doves signify the sacrifice offered in the temple by Joseph and Mary at the presentation of Christ in the temple. The three French hens, priceless poultry in 16th century England, represent the gifts of the magi.

The four calling birds are the four gospel writers. The five golden rings represent the Torah, that is, the five books of the Old Testament. The six geese a-laying signify the six days of creation; the seven swans a-swimming are the seven gifts of the Holy Spirit. The eight maids a-milking are the Beatitudes, which nourish our spirituality. The nine ladies dancing refer to the nine choirs of angels.

The ten lords-a-leaping are the Ten Commandments. The eleven pipers piping signify the eleven apostles who proclaimed the resurrection (minus Judas, who of course, was shortly there after replaced by Matthias). The twelve drummers drumming are the twelve basic beliefs enshrined in the Apostle's Creed.

So when next you hear "The Twelve Days of Christmas," maybe you can use the occasion to lift your heart and your mind to God, praying for peace in the world, and the unity of all Christians.

Arr. by Gail Smith

Repeat as necessary

six geese a laying
seven swans . . .

We Wish You A Merry Christmas

The carol was sung by a chorus of singers, called "waits," who were licensed to sing out the hours of day or night. They also sang to greet visiting dignitaries. They were especially busy during Christmas serenading on frosty evenings telling the Nativity Story in song. In return they might receive coins or a bit of fig pudding. Many of the oldest carols are "waits" carols including "We Wish You A Merry Christmas."

Arr. by Gail Smith

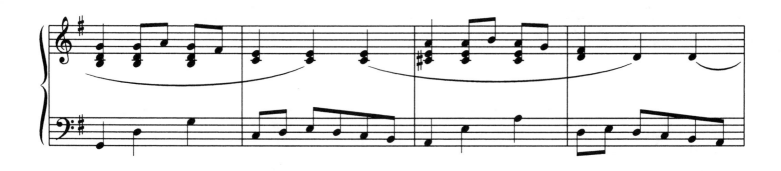

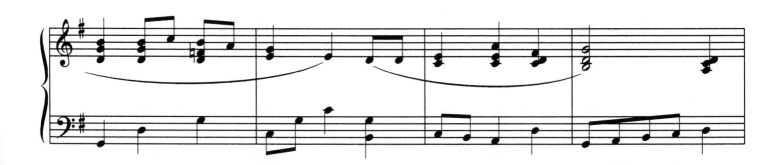